American
CULTURE & CONFLICT

Living Through
THE POST
9/11 ERA

Linden McNeilly

Rourke
Educational Media

rourkeeducationalmedia.com

Before Reading:

Building Academic Vocabulary and Background Knowledge

Before reading a book, it is important to tap into what your child or students already know about the topic. This will help them develop their vocabulary, increase their reading comprehension, and make connections across the curriculum.

1. *Look at the cover of the book. What will this book be about?*
2. *What do you already know about the topic?*
3. *Let's study the Table of Contents. What will you learn about in the book's chapters?*
4. *What would you like to learn about this topic? Do you think you might learn about it from this book? Why or why not?*
5. *Use a reading journal to write about your knowledge of this topic. Record what you already know about the topic and what you hope to learn about the topic.*
6. *Read the book.*
7. *In your reading journal, record what you learned about the topic and your response to the book.*
8. *After reading the book complete the activities below.*

Content Area Vocabulary

Read the list. What do these words mean?

casualties

coalition

evacuations

extremists

foiled

mosques

permeated

reigned

respiratory

subdued

unstable

unthinkable

After Reading:

Comprehension and Extension Activity

After reading the book, work on the following questions with your child or students in order to check their level of reading comprehension and content mastery.

1. *List and briefly explain at least three ways America was affected by the attacks on 9/11. (Summarize)*
2. *Why do you think the United States went to war so quickly after the attacks? Give several reasons. (Infer)*
3. *Think of two questions you'd ask a veteran of the war in Iraq. (Asking questions)*
4. *Have you ever felt angry toward someone you didn't know, simply because of the group they are in? Describe the situation. (Text to self connection)*
5. *Think of two questions you could ask a person of a different religion about their beliefs. (Asking questions)*

Extension Activity

Create a diary of an imaginary young person. Write at least five entries describing events after 9/11, each two years apart. Use what you know about the things that happened in the United States in the ten years from 2001 to 2011. Include details and feelings about what is going on around you.

TABLE OF CONTENTS

The Day the World Changed 4

The Long Road to Recovery 12

Terrorism: Spreading Hatred and Fear 18

Seeking Justice 32

The Rise of the Spies 38

The Way Forward 44

Glossary 46

Index 47

Show What You Know 47

Further Reading 47

About the Author 48

KEY EVENTS

September 11, 2001:	Al-Qaeda terrorist attacks occur in New York, Washington D.C., and Pennsylvania
September 20, 2001:	President George W. Bush declares "War on Terror"
October 7, 2001:	United States and allies attack Al-Qaeda bases in Afghanistan
October 26, 2001:	The U.S. Congress passes the Patriot Act, giving the government broader authority to investigate phone, email, financial, and other records
December 22, 2001:	British terrorist Richard Reid is arrested after trying to blow up an American Airlines plane with explosives hidden in his shoes, leading to requirement for shoe removal during airport security checks
November 25, 2002:	U.S. Department of Homeland Security established
March 20, 2003:	President George W. Bush sends troops to Iraq on reports of terrorism ties and weapons of mass destruction
December 13, 2003:	Iraqi President Saddam Hussein captured by U.S. military forces in Iraq
December 30, 2006:	Saddam Hussein executed after a trial that found him guilty of crimes against humanity
December 2007:	Great Recession begins
January 2, 2011:	President Barack Obama signs the James Zadroga 9/11 Health and Compensation Act into law
May 2, 2011:	9/11 mastermind Osama bin Laden killed by U.S. forces in Pakistan

CHAPTER ONE

THE DAY THE WORLD CHANGED

On September 11, 2001, terrorists flew planes into the Twin Towers at the World Trade Center and the Pentagon. A fourth plane crashed in a field in Pennsylvania. 2,977 people died in the attacks. It was the largest loss of life from a foreign attack on United States soil.

World Trade Center

A field in Pennsylvania was the crash site for the fourth plane.

Terrorists flew a plane into the Pentagon building in Washington, D.C.

This was a new kind of war. The attackers were members of Al-Qaeda, eager to kill in the name of Islamic extremism. Most Americans knew little of the enemy or their cause. Time would change that.

*Members of Al-Qaeda are Islamic **extremists**. They attacked the World Trade Center and the Pentagon because they wanted to damage the U.S. economy and military. The plane that crashed in Pennsylvania was likely headed for Washington, D. C., but the passengers joined together and **foiled** the hijackers' plans.*

The day started normally. But at 8:45 a.m., onlookers saw a jet flying toward the North Tower. The collision seemed accidental, though some noticed the plane did not appear to be in distress. The tower started burning, and **evacuations** began.

This diagram shows where planes struck the World Trade Center buildings.

Fifteen minutes later, another plane flew into the South Tower. These were not accidents. Inside, ceilings and walls fell, smashing furniture and computers. People fled to the stairwells and elevators, but some were blocked or damaged.

Rising 110 stories high, each tower had 20 elevators capable of carrying 10,000 pounds (4535.9 kilograms) at 1,600 feet (487.68 meters) per minute. Though not all elevators worked, many brought people to safety. In one stopped elevator, riders used tools to pry open the doors, hack through the sheetrock, and crawl free under a bathroom sink.

Up to 50,000 people worked at the World Trade Center buildings on a given day, but on the morning of 9/11, 14,000 people were known to be working. Most escaped.

While workers fled the damaged buildings, hundreds of police and firefighters rushed in. They helped escort or carry people out of the buildings, often going back in to look for more people in need.

Fifty-six minutes after it was hit, the South Tower fell. The North Tower, which had been hit higher up, held on for an hour and 42 minutes. The collapse of the Twin Towers damaged other buildings in the area.

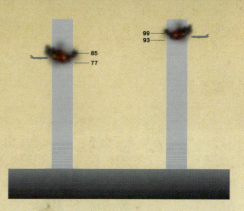

A group of 16 firefighters and business workers survived in Stairwell B in the North Tower. The entire building collapsed around them, but by a miracle of timing and luck, the stairwell stood, sheltering them. The staircase is now an important feature of the National September 11 Memorial & Museum.

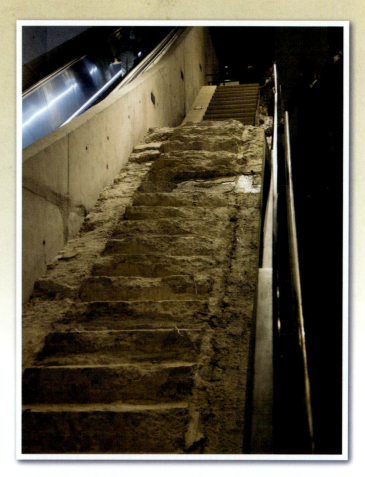

In all, 412 emergency workers—mostly firefighters—died helping others. Of the many firehouses in New York City, 75 of them lost at least one member. For months after the tragedy, communities around the country sought to honor the sacrifice by bringing baked goods, gifts, and flowers to their local firehouses.

Firefighters check for survivors after the attack.

Heartache and confusion **reigned** as frantic loved ones tried to contact those who had worked in the affected buildings, not knowing who escaped and who had not. Jammed cellphone lines made it hard for people to report that they had made it out safely.

Ladder Company 3's fire truck became part of the National September 11 Memorial & Museum, representing the men lost from that ladder company and all the New York City Fire Department **casualties**.

Since the attacks were a surprise, many New Yorkers weren't sure where to run to safety. Would attackers bomb bridges? Damage the subways? Eventually, people realized that the hijackers had intended just to hit the buildings.

Though first responders are trained to react to emergencies, the sheer size of this event was different. Many first responders who survived suffered post-traumatic stress for years. Others suffered guilt for surviving when their co-workers didn't.

A worker stands near a pile of debris at Ground Zero.

CHAPTER TWO

THE LONG ROAD TO RECOVERY

The Pentagon was seriously damaged, but recovery efforts were kept under security. The Trade Center site, renamed Ground Zero, was a focal point of recovery for months since it was at the center of one of the busiest cities in the world.

Aerial view of Ground Zero.

Workers came from all over to help at Ground Zero. At first, they hoped to find survivors, but there were few. They picked through the **unstable** debris made of concrete, steel, and rubble by hand, carefully preserving any evidence of those who perished there.

A trained rescue dog helps search for survivors and remains.

Fires burned at the center of the pile. The work was so dangerous that many police and firefighters wrote their names and phone numbers on their arms in case they fell into the pile and were crushed. But they were motivated to help by the desire to do something positive.

People rushed to donate blood and money to the Red Cross, which raised three million dollars through online donations in just two days. Donations of more than two billion dollars were eventually raised and given to various charities to support victims and their families.

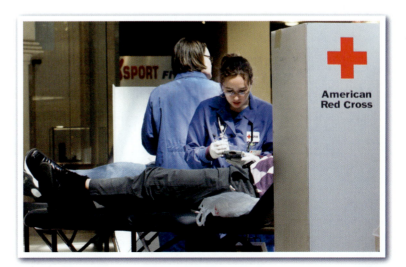

Cleanup took about a year. Eventually, handheld buckets gave way to larger equipment. Bulldozers filled trucks with 108,000 loads of rubble, placed in a Staten Island landfill, for a total of 1.8 million tons (1.6 metric tons).

The smell of burning rubber, plastic, smoke, and steel **permeated** New York City for months. Toxic dust, diesel exhaust, pulverized cement, glass fibers, and other dangerous substances floated in the air, or swirled up after moving the debris.

*Many first responders developed serious **respiratory** diseases from the conditions at Ground Zero. It took many years, but finally the James Zadroga 9/11 Health and Compensation Act became a U.S. law in 2011. It provides health monitoring and financial aid to the first responders, volunteers, and survivors of the September 11 attacks. James Zadroga was a 34-year old NYPD detective who died in 2006 of lung disease from breathing in the dust at Ground Zero. Before the law in his name was made, any injury caused by work was not covered by insurance.*

Americans were distressed. For New Yorkers, the closer to the Trade Center they lived or worked, the worse they felt. Piles of crushed metal, broken concrete, and twisted steel were daily reminders that brought waves of difficult feelings.

Two members of the New York Army National Guard stand at the World Trade Center site.

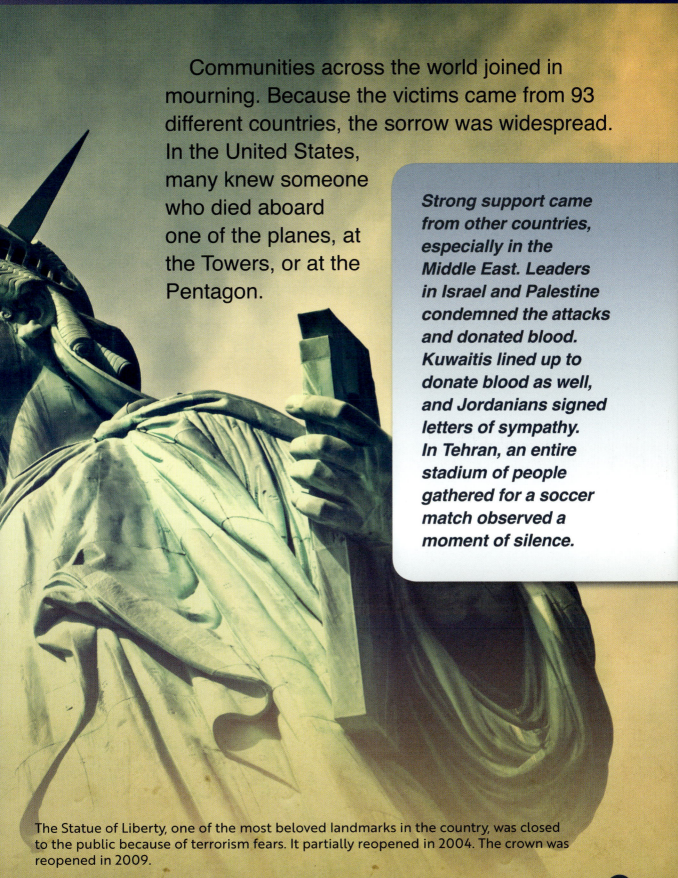

Communities across the world joined in mourning. Because the victims came from 93 different countries, the sorrow was widespread. In the United States, many knew someone who died aboard one of the planes, at the Towers, or at the Pentagon.

Strong support came from other countries, especially in the Middle East. Leaders in Israel and Palestine condemned the attacks and donated blood. Kuwaitis lined up to donate blood as well, and Jordanians signed letters of sympathy. In Tehran, an entire stadium of people gathered for a soccer match observed a moment of silence.

The Statue of Liberty, one of the most beloved landmarks in the country, was closed to the public because of terrorism fears. It partially reopened in 2004. The crown was reopened in 2009.

CHAPTER THREE

TERRORISM: SPREADING HATRED AND FEAR

Terrorism is the use of violence to scare people or governments into changing their ideas about politics, religion, or culture. Terrorists work alone or in small groups, often with a large organization that influences their ideas and directs their actions.

The 9/11 terrorists were influenced by Al-Qaeda, an extremist group whose aim was to rid the world of any non-Muslim influence. They wanted all Muslims united in an Islamic nation. They believed that killing for these beliefs is acceptable.

Terrorism has been practiced for centuries. In ancient Rome, mobs hid daggers under their robes, stabbed their enemies, then faded into the crowd. In the Middle Ages, gangs would display their enemies' severed heads on sticks to create panic. In the 1800s, the U.S. government used the random slaughter of Native Americans to evoke terror.

SAUDI ARABIA

OMAN

YEMEN

9/11 was not the first terrorist attack by Islamic extremists. The first known Al-Qaeda attack was in 1992, when a hotel in Yemen housing U.S. troops was bombed. The troops were not injured.

Terrorists want to create fear, and for a while, it worked. TV stations replayed the footage of the attacks, raising emotions. The news media published profiles of the attackers and their network, which added to feelings of unease.

Because the attackers were Arab Muslims, misinformation about Arabs, Muslims, and Islam spread quickly. Islam, a religion based on the belief in one God, and in peace and harmony in all aspects of life, was suddenly believed to be at the core of hatred and murder.

In February 1993, Ramzi Yousef, a member of Al-Qaeda, planned a truck bombing at the World Trade Center, which killed six people and injured more than a thousand.

Arabs are people who trace their ancestry to Arab nations, found in the Middle East, Africa, and on the West Indian Ocean islands. Of the 450 million Arabs worldwide, many are Muslims, believers in the religion of Islam. Some Arabs are Christians. There are 3.7 million Americans with Arab ancestry, most of them born in the United States.

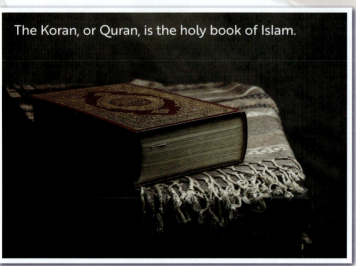

The Koran, or Quran, is the holy book of Islam.

Ignorance helped in the spread of misinformation. Though Islam is the second largest religion in the world, only one percent of the population in America follows Islam. Rumors about Islamic beliefs, most of them offensive and wrong, began quickly circulating in the media.

A surge of racism followed 9/11. Mobs attacked Islamic **mosques** and homes. Women wearing traditional headscarves and children known to be Muslim or Arab were harassed or bullied. Turban-wearers, even non-Muslims, were often targeted.

George W. Bush

President George W. Bush tried to curb the racism by visiting an Islamic mosque in Washington, D.C., saying, "Islam is peace… In our anger and emotion, our fellow Americans must treat each other with respect." But violence continued against Muslims who had nothing to do with the attacks.

Muslim parents tried to protect their children by telling them not to speak of their religion, and not to wear traditional clothing. But Muslims were still treated with violence and bigotry, even if they were born and raised in the United States.

Anytime radical Islamists attacked elsewhere, fear of Muslims would rise. Though moderate Muslims condemned the attacks, it made little difference. In the United States, racism continued to grow, as more people blamed immigrants—especially those with Arab ancestry—for their fears.

As a presidential candidate in 2016, Donald Trump proposed a "Muslim Ban" and blamed Mexicans for sending their criminals to the United States. Hate crimes, especially against Arab Americans, rose as the fear of "others" was played up for political reasons.

Donald Trump

Protesters demonstrate against anti-immigrant policies.

Patriotism spread. Flag sales exploded, with some retailers selling 25 times that of the previous year. Flags were displayed on homes, businesses, cars, and freeway overpasses. People wore flag pins or red, white, and blue T-shirts.

Patriotism gave rise to an anti-immigration movement. Securing the borders became an issue of national security. Immigrants could be seized and deported, sometimes unfairly. Legal immigration could take up to two years, requiring four different agencies' approval. Even desperate refugees were turned away.

In 2017, the Trump Administration issued a travel ban, which restricted immigrants from certain countries with higher numbers of Muslim residents. Though no known terrorists had tried to immigrate recently, the government insisted it would lead to a safer America.

A wall separates Mexico from the United States along the California border.

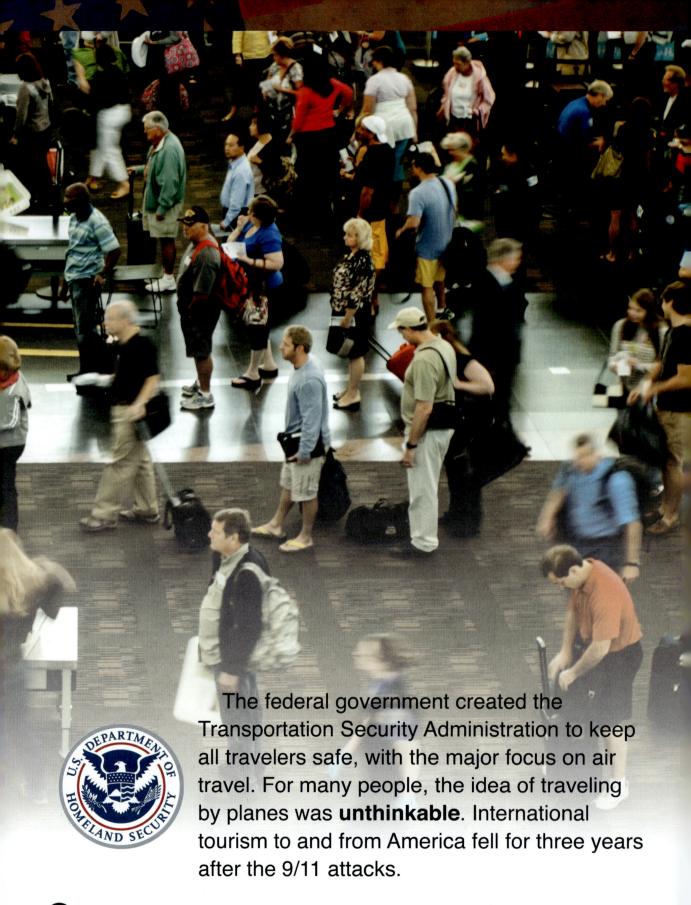

The federal government created the Transportation Security Administration to keep all travelers safe, with the major focus on air travel. For many people, the idea of traveling by planes was **unthinkable**. International tourism to and from America fell for three years after the 9/11 attacks.

Airplane travel took more time than it did before 9/11. Passengers had to wait in long security lines, endure manual searches, remove belts, watches, and other metal items. Only ticketed passengers could go to the gate.

In December 2001, a self-proclaimed British Al-Qaeda operative, Richard Reid, tried to set off a bomb with explosives packed in his shoes. Flight attendants and passengers **subdued** him. His attempt brought a new rule: airline passengers must remove their shoes before going through security.

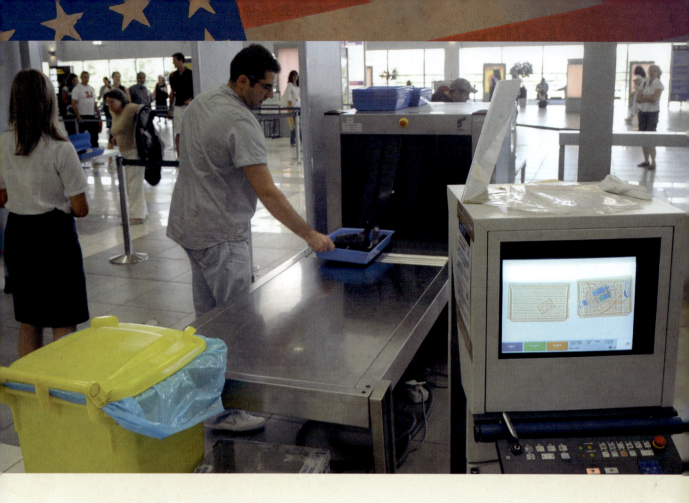

Fourteen million passengers now fly weekly to, from, and within the U.S. Every piece of checked and carried-on luggage is screened. There are more than 50 thousand transportation security officers in more than 450 airports across the country.

In 2006, British police discovered a terrorist plot to detonate liquid explosives on transatlantic aircraft from the United Kingdom to the United States and Canada. The explosives were disguised as soft drinks. As a result, no one can bring containers with more than 3.4 ounces (100 milliliters) of liquid through the security checkpoint.

Travelers may bring small quantities of liquids, gels, or pastes, but they must be in a clear, quart-sized bag.

CHAPTER FOUR

SEEKING JUSTICE

The attacks pushed the U.S. into a new kind of war, without a clear place the enemy lived. But the American people demanded action for the innocent lives lost. The government vowed to bring those who were responsible to justice.

Afghanistan's rulers, the Taliban, had allowed Al-Qaeda to train soldiers, import weapons, and plot terrorist actions. The American government demanded that the Taliban hand over Osama bin Laden, the leader of Al-Qaeda. But they refused.

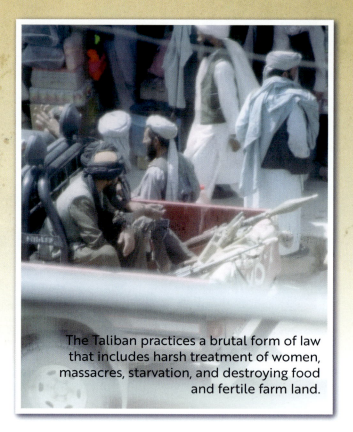

The Taliban practices a brutal form of law that includes harsh treatment of women, massacres, starvation, and destroying food and fertile farm land.

Osama bin Laden

By October 7, 2001, the United States, Britain, and Canada began to attack bases in Afghanistan known to harbor and train Al-Qaeda terrorists. Eventually, a NATO **coalition** of 40 countries joined forces to find and defeat Al-Qaeda. Though bin Laden was eventually found and killed in 2011, the war in Afghanistan has continued for 16 years and counting.

On March 20, 2003, President Bush sent troops into Iraq. He said the CIA had found weapons of mass destruction. He added that Iraq's leader, Saddam Hussein, was aiding al-Qaeda operatives.

Saddam Hussein

Many died because of these conflicts. Two million troops were sent to war between 2001 and 2011, with six thousand killed and 44 thousand wounded. Civilian death estimates in the Middle East are in the hundreds of thousands.

The cost to veterans has been high. Up to 20 percent suffer from post-traumatic stress disorder (PTSD), and 250,000 suffer from brain injury, depression, or loss of limbs.

The Battle Cross is a marker to honor a soldier who has been killed.

Though Saddam Hussein was eventually found, tried in court, and executed, no weapons of mass destruction were ever found in Iraq. Many angry Iraqis eventually became part of a new Islamic terrorist organization called The Islamic State, or ISIS.

Saddam Hussein looked ragged after he was found hiding in a hole in December 2003.

ISIS flag

ISIS members are all over the world. Their main aim is to control Syria and Iraq and rule it with extremist ideas, including killing people, especially Westerners, who do not follow their version of strict Islamic law. They use suicide bombings to kill innocent people they consider their enemies.

The New York Stock Exchange was forced to close for four days to keep people from panic selling. Stock exchanges in other parts of the world, where economies were already weak, also closed to prevent a worldwide economic catastrophe.

The U.S. economy suffered after 9/11. A two-year recession that began in March 2001 worsened. Businesses suffered from disruption, including more than a thousand at the World Trade Center alone.

Military costs added to the economic problem. The defense budget rose 31 percent from 2000 to 2014. As much as four billion dollars in military spending has gone to supporting war.

In the mid-2000s, banks made bad home loans. By 2008, the Great Recession began. Unemployment went up, with a total of 2.6 million jobs lost. Banks, car manufacturers, and consumers got temporary aid from the federal government, adding more to the debt.

The Great Recession (2007-2010) was the worst economic time in American history since the Great Depression. Wealth disappeared. Many people went long months or even years without work. Homes lost value, and businesses closed.

THE RISE OF THE SPIES

Since 9/11, approximately 200,000 people have been killed in terrorist attacks around the world. Each attack, usually a surprise that occurred in a common place such as a school, club or market, was designed to raise fear.

The rapid spread of online news coverage of attacks raises fears, which contributes to racism.

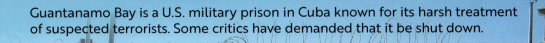
Guantanamo Bay is a U.S. military prison in Cuba known for its harsh treatment of suspected terrorists. Some critics have demanded that it be shut down.

Congress passed the controversial Patriot Act soon after 9/11. The government could hold suspects indefinitely, search homes and businesses without permission, and access phone, email, and financial records without a court order. But many of these provisions were challenged in court and found unconstitutional.

While many Americans protested the increased spying, others were willing to give up their rights to privacy for the sense of security. Since no further large-scale attacks have happened on American soil, many people are convinced that the new rules offer them better security.

Cybersecurity went international. The government made agreements with other countries to share information about terrorists or criminals. Code breakers and double agents gathered secrets from the enemy abroad.

One significant governmental change after 9/11 was the establishment of the Department of Homeland Security (DHS). It combined 22 government agencies. It manages border security, emergency response, and cybersecurity, along with Customs, the U.S. Coast Guard, and the Transportation Security Administration.

The DHS's 240,000 employees do many things. Some work on strategies to limit biological weapon use against the U.S. Others provide emergency services during natural disasters, like fires or floods. Others patrol the borders and check those who enter the country.

U.S. Immigration and Customs Enforcement

Government workers try to think like terrorists to predict and prevent attacks. Police presence is increased at historical landmarks. When many important people gather, security is heightened.

HOMELAND SECURITY ADVISORY SYSTEM

SEVERE
SEVERE RISK OF TERRORIST ATTACKS

HIGH
HIGH RISK OF TERRORIST ATTACKS

ELEVATED
SIGNIFICANT RISK OF TERRORIST ATTACKS

GUARDED
GENERAL RISK OF TERRORIST ATTACKS

LOW
LOW RISK OF TERRORIST ATTACKS

Some areas have new requirements for security. Large cargo containers arriving on ships, previously only spot-checked for drugs or weapons, now must undergo close screening.

"If you see something, say something," became a slogan to raise the public's awareness of potential safety threats.

For the first time, local, state, tribal, and federal authorities shared a database with information on suspected terrorists and criminals. Local police were trained to recognize behaviors related to terrorism. Urban centers shared information on threats to public safety.

The Joint Terrorism Task Forces, which consist of federal, state, and local law enforcement officers working across the country, tripled from 2001 to 2016. The groups run drills and help state and local authorities plan for emergencies.

While law enforcement increased their focus on possible terrorists, many innocent people, especially those of color, were wrongly accused of crimes they didn't commit. Immigrants or citizens with ancestry that seemed "suspicious" were often the targets of raids or arrests.

CHAPTER SIX

THE WAY FORWARD

Many things changed in America on September 11, 2001. In some ways, Americans traded their idealism for suspicion and fear. But many citizens and leaders are working hard to keep fairness and justice at the forefront of political discussions.

The Internet has added to the rapid spread of extremist ideas. But social pressure has forced some social media companies to take greater measures to stop the use of their sites for recruiting extremists. Social media has also kept people informed on current events and helped groups make positive changes.

Terrorists hoped to ruin the American economy and devastate the country. Though times have been hard, and challenges still lie ahead, they were not entirely successful. The fact that Americans still openly debate and air differences is testament to the strength of the nation's democracy.

The "Tribute in Light" is a memorial to the Twin Towers.

The National September 11 Memorial & Museum exhibition at the Twin Towers site features artifacts, images, first-person testimony, and archival audio and video recordings to retell the story of the events of September 11, 2001.

GLOSSARY

casualties (KAZH-oo-uhl-tees): people injured or killed in war

coalition (koh-uh-LISH-uhn): a group formed for a common purpose

evacuations (i-VAK-yoo-ay-shuns): movements away from a dangerous area

extremists (ik-STREE-mists): people who have extreme views, usually about religion or politics

foiled (foild): prevented from doing something

mosques (mahsks): buildings where Muslims worship

permeated (PUR-mee-ate-id): spread throughout something

reigned (rayned): was widespread

respiratory (RES-pur-uh-tor-ee): having to do with breathing in and out

subdued (sub-DOOD): quiet and less active

unstable (uhn-STAY-buhl): likely to fall apart or get worse

unthinkable (UHN-thing-kuh-buhl): so unlikely or undesirable that it cannot be considered or imagined

INDEX

Afghanistan 32

Al-Qaeda 5, 19, 21, 29

Bush, George 23

bin Laden, Osama 32

Ground Zero 12, 13, 15

Islam 21, 22, 23

Muslim 19, 21, 22, 23, 24,25, 27

Patriot Act 39

patriotism 26, 27

Pentagon 4, 5, 12, 17

racism 23, 25, 38

Taliban 32

Twin Towers 4, 9, 45

World Trade Center 4, 5, 7,16, 21, 36

Zadroga, James 15

SHOW WHAT YOU KNOW

1. Explain why the terrorists chose the World Trade Center and the Pentagon as two of the targets for their attack.

2. What made the attack such a difficult experience for first responders?

3. What kinds of feelings lead to racism? Give several examples and explain.

4. How has the Internet changed the way extremist views are shared?

5. What can individual people do to reduce terrorism?

FURTHER READING

Rhodes, Jewel Parker, *Towers Falling*, Little, Brown Books for Young Readers, 2016.

January, Brendan, *Isis, the Global Face of Terrorism*, Twenty First Century Books, 2017.

Ghobash, Omar Saif, *Letters to a Young Muslim*, Picador 2017.

ABOUT THE AUTHOR

Linden McNeilly is a writer who taught public school for many years. She loves writing about history, science, interesting places to go, and maps. She lives in the redwoods of California with her family and lots of pets. Visit her at www.lindenmcneilly.com.

www.rourkeeducationalmedia.com

Photo Credits: Cover: tower By Alexander Prokopenko, flags By Janece Flippo; page 4-5 pentagon © Everett Historical, twin towers © Dan Howell; page 6-7 North tower Twin Towers © Ken Tannenbaum, towers before attack © robert paul van beets; page 8-9 © Anthony Correia; page 10-11 ladder 3 © Antonio Gravante; red cross © littlenySTOCK; page 17 © Delpixel; page 18-19 silhouetted figure © Prazis Images, map © Harvepino; page 20-21 map © Peter Hermes Furian; page 22-23 muslim prayer © Titima Ongkantong, koran © kamomeen, protestors © arindambanerjee; page 24 © a katz, page 25 Islam Means Peace © Morgan Rauscher; page 26 flag © Naypong; page 28-29 long lines © Arina P Habich, TSA wand © Carolina K. Smith MD, shoes etc. © trekandshoot; page 30-31 luggage screening © bibiphoto, airplane © tishomir, plastic bag © Monkey Business Images; page 32-33 map © Ingo Menhard, page 36-37 Stock Exchange © ventdusud, stock exchange small photo © By Stuart Monk, businessman © Pcess609, page 38-39 congress © Rob Crandall, people using cell phones © GaudiLab, computers © Gorodenkoff; page 40-41 border wall © Sherry V Smith, customs form © danielfela; cargo ship © Sheila Fitzgerald; page 42-43 computer map © © Semisatch, page 42-43 man in hand cuffs © sirtravelalot; page 44-45 city lights © Mike Ver Sprill, page 45 © rarrarorro   All images from Shuuterstock.com except: page 4-5 Pennsylvania crash site courtesy of U.S. Government, background photo and page 10-11 Ground Zero and page 14-15 first responders courtesy of Mike Goad; page 6-7 map courtesy FEMA, page 8-9 © Mark Kent   https://creativecommons.org/licenses/by-sa/2.0/deed.en ; page 10-11 firefighters courtesy of Library of Congress, lone firefighter courtesy of U.S. Navy; page 12-13 K-9 rescue Andrea Booher/ FEMA News Photo, satellite view NASA, aerial view of building U.S. Navy; page 14-15 "bucket brigade" courtesy of U.S. Navy; page 16-17 National Guard courtesy FEMA; page 20-21Newseum - 911 Front Pages Wide © Davis Staedtler   https://creativecommons.org/licenses/by/2.0/deed.en ; page 26-27 ICE officer courtesy of U.S. Government, border wall Rev Sysyphus at English Wikipedia; page 34 soldiers courtesy of U.S. Army, soldier's cross © James McCauley https://creativecommons.org/licenses/by/2.0/deed.en ; page 40-41 boat courtesy of U.S. Government

Edited by: Keli Sipperley

Produced by Blue Door Education for Rourke Educational Media. Cover and Interior design by: Jennifer Dydyk

Living Through the Post 9/11 Era / Linden McNeilly
(American Culture and Conflict)
 ISBN 978-1-64156-420-5 (hard cover)
 ISBN 978-1-64156-546-2 (soft cover)
 ISBN 978-1-64156-669-8 (e-Book)
Library of Congress Control Number: 2018930441